IMAGES
of England

HEYSHAM

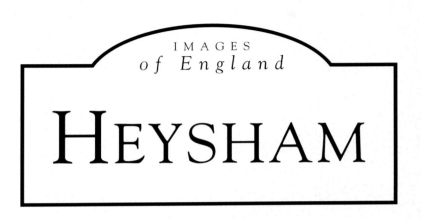

IMAGES
of England

HEYSHAM

Compiled by David Flaxington
for Heysham Heritage Association

TEMPUS

Heysham Point, the best-known natural landmark on the Lancashire coast.

Frontispiece: Stone stairway in the Rectory Wood. One of Heysham's many ancient and intriguing features.

First published 2002

Tempus Publishing Limited
The Mill, Brimscombe Port,
Stroud, Gloucestershire, GL5 2QG

British Library Cataloguing in Publication Data.
A catalogue record for this book is available from the British Library.

ISBN 0 7524 2680 X

Typesetting and origination by Tempus Publishing Limited
Printed in Great Britain by Midway Colour Print, Wiltshire

Contents

Acknowledgements

Thanks must go first to Rex Wilmshurst for the loan of his superb collection of old postcards of which only a sample selection are shown here. The postcards present a visual record of Heysham from the turn of the nineteenth/twentieth centuries to the 1960s, while the more recent photographs and other items have been included to complete the picture and bring the record up to date.

Despite the declining fortunes of most British coastal resorts, the timeless and unchanging character of Heysham Village is clearly evident throughout. Many thanks, therefore, must go to the National Trust, Heysham Neighbourhood Council, St Peter's Church and all other organizations and individuals both past and present whose efforts have ensured that Heysham Village has retained its familiar characteristics – picturesque, tranquil and unhurried most of the time, but able to burst into life whenever the occasion demands.

Thanks also to the Royds, Rawesthornes, Mashiters, Hutchinsons, Lathams, Hadaths, and other Heysham families whose legacies remain either as visual reminders of Heysham's past, or as happy memories which linger to this day in the minds of so many. Not to be forgotten, of course, are all the Gerties, Florries, Maggies, Alices and all the other lasses and lads from Yorkshire and beyond who visited Heysham and sent postcards home to their friend and families.

This book is the brainchild of Barbara Verhoef and John Holding, Secretary and Chairman of Heysham Heritage Association, without whose dedication projects such as this would never see the light of day (see chapter nine, contributed by John Holding).

David Flaxington

Foreword

by John Holding, Chairman of
Heysham Heritage Association

Heysham has a very long and intriguing history to which many publications, including this one, testify. Heysham Heritage Association has published a number of books on the local history but none have been quite like this. When David Buxton of Tempus Publishing visited Heysham two years ago, his proposal to publish a book about Heysham based on postcards from Rex Wilmshurst's collection was very warmly welcomed.

At the time David Flaxington was busy completing his own *History of Heysham* (now published by the Association) but when this was finished we were delighted to find that he was ready to undertake the painstaking task of compiling this postcard archive, together with other photographs, into a well-organized format, complete with appropriate and informative captions. We congratulate him on a superb result, and commend the book to all lovers of Heysham.

Introduction

Before the arrival of the Romans, the inhabitants of the Morecambe Bay area appear to have been a mixture of both Celts and pre-Celts. It is believed that as the incoming Celtic settlers moved further north and west pushing Britain's earlier inhabitants before them, these indigenous people made their final stand around Morecambe Bay. Instead of being wiped out by the Celts, the two somehow managed to coexist until they eventually became a mixed race.

Evidence suggests that the Chapel Hill area above Heysham Village has been an important centre of religious activity since these earliest times.

Because of this the inhabitants of Heysham, despite the area's isolated location, have made the acquaintance over the years of Roman traders and legionnaires from Lancaster, monks from Ireland, Anglian settlers from Northumbria, Norwegian Vikings from the Isle of Man, and finally Norman lords and land barons.

In Anglo-Saxon times Northumbria was ruled from York. When Anglian settlers from the east extended the border of Northumbria as far as the west coast, North Lancashire became a part of Yorkshire. The Domesday entry for Heysham states 'Heysham, land of the King in Yorkshire'.

In a recent interpretation of the Domesday Book (published by Coombe Books: editor Thomas Hinde) the additional commentary states:

'There is no way of telling where the brash resort of Morecambe ends and the town of Heysham begins, but they were once two distinct places. Holiday-makers who grow tired of Morecambe's sand and slot machines can drive a couple of miles south and suddenly find themselves in a corner of old England almost too quaint to be true. Old Heysham is not entirely untouched by modern Morecambe, however. There is Heysham rock, candy floss and a shop that claims to sell the largest selection of fudges in Lancashire. The eighteenth-century buildings along the little main street are genuine, and the two churches which stand side by side on the rocks above the beach are more venerable than donkey rides and even the Domesday itself.'

Unfortunately today there are no more donkey rides! Since the advent of the continental package holiday, family resorts such as Morecambe have been plunged into a state of almost terminal decline. Today's holidaymakers have abandoned the traditional two weeks by the English seaside in favour of cut-price trips to the Costa's and beyond, for sun, sangria, bad plumbing, questionable cuisine and the inevitable touch of the 'Calcutta quick-step'.

Those who still choose to visit the Morecambe Bay area, however, realized long ago that the things that really matter have not changed. Morecambe's four miles of promenade offers the same unspoilt and often spectacular views of the distant mountains, and at the foot of the rolling hills directly across the bay Grange-over-Sands and other tiny villages still sprawl lazily in the afternoon sun.

In the evenings the ever-changing mood of the sky still offers an endless variety of glorious sunsets, the effects of which are often more spectacular when viewed from the nearby village of

Heysham. It has been justifiably claimed that from Heysham's Chapel Hill, where the ancient ruins overlook the breathtaking panorama of Morecambe Bay, on a clear day you really can see forever!

Anyone seeking the traditional pleasures associated with a visit to the seaside – pubs, cafés, shops and markets, sun, sand and ice cream – will even today find themselves well satisfied at Heysham, while those of a different nature can enjoy a welcome respite from the daily turmoil and the pressures of daily life by simply gazing out at the soul-calming vastness of sea and sky, or by lingering for a while in the quiet tree-shrouded serenity of St Peter's churchyard.

In addition to these diverse attractions, at Heysham thousands of years of English history is still in evidence, captured forever in silent stone for all to see and touch and walk amongst. Within the space of a few hundred square yards to which the public has free access are many mysterious features which have baffled historians and inflamed the imagination of generations of casual observers.

On a rocky promontory adjacent to St Patrick's chapel are the enigmatic rock-hewn graves (or stone coffins) of unknown antiquity, while in the nearby Rectory Wood a huge hollowed-out stone is claimed by tradition to be a Druidic sacrificial altar. Close by stands what is believed to be a megalithic tomb. Not far away in the grounds of St Peter's Church can be found the elaborately carved base of an Anglian cross (from around AD 700), while other ancient crosses and gravestones lean precariously all around.

Apart from these visible reminders of Heysham's ancient past, at the foot of the nearby Barrows an archaeological dig unearthed over 1,000 Mesolithic artefacts, indicating that this area was home to some of Britain's earliest inhabitants as far back as 10,000 BC.

Although unbelievably neglected over the years by most mainstream archaeologists and historians, the ancient and sometimes turbulent history of this incredibly quaint and picturesque part of the Lancashire coastline will continue to be preserved and documented by Heysham Heritage Association.

This book is based upon a superb collection of old postcards owned by Rex Wilmshurst, an Association member. Some more recent photographs have been included wherever relevant.

One
Ancient and Mysterious
Places

The Grandeur of Morecambe Bay as seen from Heysham's Chapel Hill.

A stubborn local legend claims that St Patrick's Chapel, one of Heysham's most popular features, was built by St Patrick and his followers after they were shipwrecked at Heysham. Although showing a few cracks as a result of certain archaeological conclusions, the legend endures, having become an intrinsic part of Heysham folklore.

The mysterious rock-hewn graves have so far defied all attempts to date them accurately. They were once believed to have been connected in some way with St Patrick's Chapel, but recent evidence suggests that they pre-date the chapel and may even date from the earliest occupation of the site.

Several of Heysham's past rectors appear to have been fanatical restorers, renovators and general 'tidier-uppers' of ancient sites and properties, making it difficult for anyone other than a professional archaeologist to determine where some ancient stonework ends and more recent work begins. St Patrick's Chapel, however, is an exception, as the restored parts are clearly discernible. The two views here are of this ancient chapel before the restoration work had been carried out.

St Peter's Church, originally a crude barn-shaped structure, is believed to have been built by Anglian settlers about the same time as St Patrick's chapel (around AD 700). Little evidence of this exists today however, as the church has been restored and extended several times, first by the Normans and later by succeeding rectors. The original Anglian doorway was preserved for posterity by Revd John Royds (rector of Heysham Parish 1858-1865) who had it removed from the church and rebuilt stone by stone in the church grounds.

The original Anglian doorway of St Peter's Church.

Throughout Britain many once-familiar town centres and even whole villages have fallen victim to the developer's bulldozer. At Heysham architectural styles, technological advancements, fads and fashions have come and gone, yet the tiny village (a Conservation Area since 1972) has survived virtually unscathed. While outlying parts of Greater Heysham have become a property developer's paradise, Heysham Village has stood aloof and indifferent to it all, and remains a welcoming oasis of calm in a frantic world – as typified by these two views of St Peter's Church taken one hundred years apart.

Although this Anglian cross-base dates from the time of the original St Peter's Church, the term 'Anglian' may be confusing to those who have previously seen Heysham's ancient structures referred to by Victorian writers as 'Saxon'. The Victorians, who in other respects were diligent historians, appear to have been genuinely unaware of the existence of the Angles of Northumbria. Apart from the Celts everyone and everything in England from the time of the departure of the Romans was referred to by the Victorians as 'Saxon'.

This ancient causeway, unknown, unnoticed and unmentioned even by Heysham's residents, runs from the edge of the Barrows into the little bay beside Throbshaw Point.

The story goes that the rector of the day, after sensing an evil presence inside the Old Rectory (*above and right*), carried all the furniture, fittings, paintings, tapestries and religious artefacts into the rectory grounds and set fire to them. He then went back indoors and set fire to the rectory itself. Evil, according to ancient religious mythology, can only be purged by flame. Following this the present rectory was built.

The lady who once kept house for the rector claims that at the rear of the rectory was an older part, the door to which was always kept locked. On the few occasions she had looked inside, she had found the place to be damp and dismal, with a certain uncomfortable feeling about it. This lady had retired by the time the above incident is alleged to have taken place and has no knowledge of it. No other substantiating evidence has been uncovered.

15

The Rectory Wood, sometimes dark and foreboding, sometimes beautiful, always mysterious.

Now known as the Rectory Wood (although the trees are of comparatively recent origin) this eighteenth-century rectory garden is believed to have once been a Druidic ceremonial area. The pathways all lead ultimately to an area in which no vegetation grows. Around this area are several strange and so far unexplained ancient features.

A recent topographic survey of the Rectory Wood, although painstakingly detailed from a visual point of view, resulted in a curious mixture of scientific observation and academic guesswork which raised more questions than the surveyors could provide answers to. Here the Royal Hotel in Heysham Village can be seen from the 'ceremonial area'.

The popular image of the High Priest standing over the sacrificial altar, his ceremonial knife raised high over the heart of a terrified victim, is an image created by Hollywood and propagated by Hammer Films. Here in the Rectory Wood the Druid's victim, after having a sword or spear thrust into the back, would hopefully have been dead when placed upon the altar for the final part of the ceremony.

This incredibly well-preserved reminder of Heysham's ancient past dates from the time when Norwegian Vikings from the Isle of Man settled the coastal area of north Lancashire and Cumbria. In order to protect the carvings from the ravages of time and weather, and the unwelcome attention of vandals, the stone now rests safely inside the church.

Two
Main Street

Even in the depth of winter Heysham Village retains its gentle and timeless qualities.

Heysham's later history is preserved in the lingering 'Olde Worlde' charm of Main Street where seventeenth/eighteenth-century cottages, barns and converted cow 'ship-ons', surround the early sixteenth-century Royal Hotel. Built in 1502 as a grain store, the main building of the Royal Hotel is the oldest property in Heysham (with the exception of St Peter's Church). Standing in the doorway of her cottage, adjacent to the Royal Hotel, is little 'Granny' Hutchinson selling her famous nettle drink (later known as nettle beer) at 2p a glass. Although made by others and still sold in Heysham Village this refreshing drink was brewed originally from an age-old Hutchinson family recipe. The Hutchinsons are a well-known Heysham family. Two of Granny's sons worked at Heysham's Bobbin Mill until its closure; one of her grandsons became the local cobbler and shoemaker with premises in Woborrow Road; another was killed during the Second World War in the first airborne attack on Arnhem; a third, Charlie, became a merchant seaman. Later Charlie worked on the harbour ferries and served on every tugboat in the entire fleet, including the once-famous *Wyvern*.

A recent photograph of the beautifully preserved Royal Hotel. As a grain store this property stood alone on the edge of an extensive area of agricultural land. Little is known about the building's history until February 1922 when the property was conveyed to Messrs A. and J.F. Barker, brewers of Lancaster. It was already a public house tenanted by Mr John Pearson, who was also a farmer.

By 1940 the brewing of nettle drink had spread to several other properties. Although built in 1627, the cottage pictured here still exists. The tiny extension was added four years later. The taller building, about which little is known, obviously dates from an earlier period as the cottage and extension have clearly been built against it.

Heysham Village.

An extract from St Peter's School log book states that: 'on 25 August 1892 school closed on Thursday afternoon and all day on Friday, that parents of children might attend a garden party at the Rectory to meet Mr and Mrs Otley. Children's treat on Friday'.

Judging from the postcard above and the recent photograph below, it seems that although the stage was set over a century ago, since then only the players have changed! Heysham Heritage Centre is on the right of the photograph.

Two almost identical views of Main Street. Almost identical, but not quite! As Heysham moved reluctantly into a new era (before the village became a Conservation Area) the cottage in the centre was demolished and replaced by a more imposing semi-detached property. 'It could have been worse...' villagers have been heard to remark, 'At least it's not a multi-storey car park!'

Greese House (or Cottage) pictured here in 1906, is believed to have been built around 1664. The actual date is uncertain as a stone on the outside bears the date 1680, while one of the main beams inside the house is inscribed with the date 1657. As the first stone-built property to be occupied by Heysham's rectors, the main building is popularly referred to as The Old Rectory. The term 'greese' derives from the Latin word *gradus* meaning 'steps', the main door being reached by a flight of seven steps.

Greese House today.

This card with its heartfelt message was sent in 1947 by a mother to her son, Corporal J.L. Riley, A Squadron, 3rd Royal Tank Regiment, BAOR: 'Dear Leslie, Dad and I got here about 3 p.m. and have just had a meal at Heysham at that place we used to get strawberries and cream – remember – in the little alcove, and we have walked here along Morecambe front. It is lovely to know you will soon be here too. Love, Mother and Dad.' Let's hope he made it!

A recent photograph of the row of fine old terraced cottages seen above. Built in 1721.

Heysham Village.

Known locally as 'The Manor House', No. 4 Main Street, pictured here in 1904, was occupied for some time by Revd John Royds while the old rectory was being restored and extended. The property appears to have acquired the title Manor House because of this. From the fifteenth century Heysham's rectors inherited, or acquired by other means, so much land and so many properties that each succeeding rector was regarded as 'lord of the manor of Lower Heysham'.

Number 4 Main Street today.

A *History of Lancashire* published shortly after the construction Heysham Harbour states: 'Lower Heysham, in spite of recent changes, remains a picturesque village with many quaint houses. In recent times the healthiness of the place has attracted many summer visitors. The ancient churches are visited by many of those who spend their summer holidays in Morecambe and its neighbourhood.'

One of Morecambe's summer visitors spent a few hours at Heysham in 1939 and sent this postcard home: 'Dear Mother and Father, the weather is lovely today. We have been to Heysham this morning and it was lovely. We are going to Grange this afternoon. Beats work any time. Love, Olive.'

By the end of the nineteenth century the glebe lands at Heysham covered over ninety acres. The sale of produce and the rents from church-owned lands and properties, plus the financial returns from tithes, enabled men of the cloth to amass their own private fortunes. Today's image of the local rector pottering around his parish and fussing over his parishioners was a long way into the future. Since the demise of these less-than-heavenly practices all that remains of Heysham's glebe land is this secluded little garden, created by the voluntary efforts of local people.

This view of lower Main Street, with the Glebe Garden on the right, is a little unusual. Snow falls on Heysham as it does elsewhere of course, but with the fresh saline breeze blowing in from Morecambe Bay and the Irish Sea, the snow usually melts as quickly as it settles. Christmas card scenes such as this are rare!

Main Street in the 'swinging sixties' looks little different, apart from the fashions, than it did in the not-so-swinging thirties. This postcard was sent by George to his friends in Watford, after a brief visit to Heysham: 'Dear Rene and Stan, Well, we arrived quite safe. We got into Lancaster at 1.10 p.m. I am just going to see Mr and Mrs Walmesley now, and then going back to the County (in Lancaster) for a beer. Cheerio.'

Parish Council rate books from the nineteenth century note that the Royd's, and one or two other major land owners, each paid between three and four hundred pounds per annum in an age when a week's wages could be reckoned in shillings and pence. Along with many other properties in Heysham, Yew Tree Cottage on Main Street, viewed here from the church entrance, is believed to have been owned at one time by the Royd's, as was the adjacent property, Barrows House.

The telephone, invented by Scottish-born Alexander Graham Bell, was patented in the USA in 1875. Heysham's first telephone was installed in Timperley's Newsagent and Tobacconist shop at No. 48 Main Street.

One of Heysham's popular weekend pageants passing Timperley's Newsagent's shop (extreme left). These pageants are so familiar today that no-one seems able to remember when or for what purpose this one was staged.

Three
Village Centre

Heysham's rush-hour shoppers hurrying home with the week's groceries.

This card, posted in 1904 to Miss A. Thornley in the village of Westhoughton near Bolton, highlights the casual regard many people had for the security of their property in the days when, as far as village people were concerned, burglary and common theft were virtually unknown, and trains left precisely on time: 'Dear Annie, We didn't come on the 9 past 6, we came on the 2.30 and we arrived about 5 o'clock. You might try our front door and see if it is locked. If so let me know as I was in a hurry.'

This card was sent to Mrs Millar of No. 5 Wellington Street, Nelson: 'Dear Friend, Hope you arrived home alright last week. It was nice having you. We are enjoying our stay at Crag Bank. Nellie says she is feeling better. We have had nice weather so far. Today is lovely, plenty of sunshine. Love and all good wishes, Clara.'

A wonderful shot of the village smithy at work in 1908. Ethel from Halifax in Yorkshire appears to have craved a little more excitement: 'Arrived safely about 6 o'clock. It has been a beautiful day, but very quiet. Hope to hear from you soon.'

One year later, in 1909, again not everyone is overjoyed: 'Dear Father, We all hope you arrived home in good health and spirits this evening. I am glad to say that 'Ma' is keeping quite well. We spent the evening after you left in the [unreadable], but am sorry to say were not all struck with it.'

Evelyn, writing to Mr A. Sharwood of Sheffield on 15 September 1924, appears to have enjoyed her visit to Heysham on Carnival Day, the previous Friday: 'My dear Alfred, Just a card to say we are still OK and still waiting for a few lines. We went to this place on Friday and had a grand time. The carnival was fine, and so is the weather.'

The writer of this card, posted on 4 August 1938, seems equally satisfied: 'The weather is very good indeed and hope it will continue. We are enjoying our holiday and are quite sunburnt.'

In early photographs of Lower Heysham the village post office is situated on the left at the entrance to Main Street. By the time this postcard appeared, the post office had moved to the corner of Woborrow Road. Today's post office occupies premises in the centre of this photograph at the corner of Main Street and Bailey Lane.

Today's post office premises are seen here to be F.W. and L. Rogers' all-purpose store. In this photograph the property just in view at the entrance to Woborrow Road (extreme right) is a sub-office of Morecambe's local newspaper, *The Visitor*, which in the 1930s incorporated *The Heysham Chronicle*.

THE HEYSHAM CHRONICLE
July 13th, 1938.

HEYSHAM BOWLER SCARES BATSMEN

They Scored Only 4 Runs Off Him in 13 Overs

How Brook & Kershaw's Lost

Heysham (h) 115, Brook & Kershaws 38

SO deadly was the bowling of A. Wilson for Heysham on Saturday that he scared Brook and Kershaw's batsmen, who scored only four singles off him in 13 overs. He took three wickets for four runs.

J. Hilton also bowled well, taking seven wickets for 34 runs, with the result that the visitors never looked like making a big score and were all out for only 38 in reply to Heysham's total of 115.

Top scorer for Heysham was J. Kitchen with 28, while F. Kitchen scored 21 and W. Birtle 20. In bowling Heysham were excellent, in batting sound, and in fielding smart. They did not yield a single extra.

J. Levett gave a good account of himself for the Builders, being next to top scorer with nine and taking three wickets for 16 runs. R. Kitchen took three for 13.

Those were the days!

Four
Halls, Old Halls, Pubs, Cafés and Cottages

Fishermen's cottages opposite the Royal Hotel, Main Street.

Happy Memories of Heysham.

Happy memories indeed, obviously from a gentler age. The building on the left was originally the farmhouse to Carr House Farm, built by the farm's owners, Richard Hodgson and his wife Elizabeth (Mashiter). The village car park, recreational area and cricket field now occupy part of the original farm land. The farm was inherited by the Mashiter family, who later rented the farmhouse to the Lancaster and District Co-operative Society to be converted into the village 'Co-op Shop'. In 1923 the Co-operative Society vacated the premises to build a new shop with a house attached (seen here on the right). This property is now Curiosity Corner. The vacant farm building was rented again, this time to become the Central Café, which for many years catered to the holidaymakers who flocked into the village on their way to and from the entertainment park on Heysham Head. When the Mashiter's finally sold the property it was converted into a Chinese restaurant, later to become the Jade Palace owned by Hong Kong businessman Mr Jimmy Chan.

38

The larger building on the right is the Village Institute. This property was given to Heysham Parish on the occasion of Queen Victoria's Diamond Jubilee in 1897 by Revd Charles Twemlow Royds. The property consisted originally of a coach house, two stables and a barn, so to raise funds for its conversion into a library and reading room a committee was appointed.

One of the Institute's original committee members was Mr Thomas Mashiter, well-known local councillor and land owner, and a member of Heysham's longest-surviving resident family. Related to the Mashiters is Mrs B. Tollitt of No. 26 Bailey Lane. This property was built in 1707 when part of the building (now No. 24) was used for wool combing.

Heysham, seen here from the 'Back o' Town centre', seems little changed since the following description: 'A prettier composition of scenery of a simple and placid character I have seldom seen. The cottages are disposed without any formality at various elevations on the side of a steep bank, with small gardens and orchards amongst them, and honeysuckle creeping around the doors and casements.' (*The Saturday Magazine*, 3 December 1836)

A few years later however, no longer does little Jimmy hurry home with his sparking clogs and his basket of mussels for the family table. Instead high-class tea rooms offer high-class confectionery to the 'opulent and well-dressed people who were attracted to Heysham by the superiority of the accommodations.'

In tea rooms or gardens the English cuppa reigns supreme, give or take the odd cup of coffee, Horlicks or Ovaltine. In Latham's Tea Gardens, however, a cup of Horlicks or Ovaltine would have been regarded as not only inappropriate, but downright sacrilegious.

In a manner typical of those freed from drudgery for a week or two, working girl Peggy, while relaxing in Hadath's Tea Gardens in the grounds if the Old Rectory (Greese House), kicks a little sand into the faces of her workmates at Sheldons, Parker-Lang, Burnley: 'Enjoying myself very much. The weather is glorious today. I am sat in the Tea Gardens writing this. Don't work too hard. See you soon.'

Standing beside the entrance to the Cliff Footpath and café, this sturdy old property was once the farmhouse to Salem Farm. Part of the farmland is now home to Salem Mews, a picturesque little private estate.

From the early nineteenth century, the much-acclaimed 'salubrity of the air' encouraged the sick to visit Heysham to recuperate. The lady on the left setting off for a stroll along the Cliff Footpath may well have been one of them, as the writer of this postcard, sent in 1924 to Green Bank near Oldham, appears to have been: 'Dear Mrs Roberts, Just a line to say I am sure you will be alright here. I have been very ill but I hope to get better soon. Love to you.'

The Cliffs café has been relocated and the seating area extended since the days of Walker's Hut, but although quite busy during the summer months, the café has never been allowed to exceed its potential.

This incredibly old view of Heysham Village, before the Cliff Footpath existed, was printed in Germany. The land from Woborrow Terrace (lower Knowlys Road) to the cliff edge belonged to Robert Swindlehurst of Salem Farm.

Like so many of Heysham's older properties these quaint cottages in Carr Lane have stood the test of time and have remained virtually unchanged since the seventeenth century. The term Carr (or Scarr) derives from a term used by Heysham's Norwegian Viking settlers to describe an area of precipitous rock. This rock still exists above Carr Lane although newer properties have since been constructed upon it.

Crimewell Lane was known originally as Heysham Hill before the properties beyond these were constructed. The blacksmith's shop (extreme right), seen in most early views of the village centre, no longer exists.

Heysham Village as seen from Crimewell Lane, in the days when Heysham catered to 'high class' visitors who unfortunately were 'more select than numerous'. The hotel on the left (built in 1903) still exists, although not as a hotel.

The village centre today from lower Crimewell Lane. The end property on the left was once the King's Arms Hotel. Guests entered through the front door while the Public Bar entrance was in Carr Lane at the rear of the hotel. This part of the property is separately owned.

When the manor of Heysham was created there were five areas within the Greater Manor; Little Heysham (the low land from the Battery to Cross Cop), Upper Heysham (Cross Cop to Heysham Towers), Nether Heysham (towards Heysham Moss), Lower Heysham (the area around the village) and Over Heysham (from Heysham Towers to the border of Middleton). Higher Heysham, with its own village and church, is a later term and denotes the area where Heysham's most important citizens and biggest landowners dwelt. These two delightful views of Old Middleton Road, Higher Heysham, show a long-forgotten ivy-covered archway leading to a private estate.

The quiet charm of Old Middleton Road today. Heysham House (below) built in 1810 by the Tatham family, was once owned by Heysham-born MP for Preston, Sir William Tomlinson Bart., who died in 1912 leaving his sister still in residence. Later, this fine old Georgian property was occupied by Alderman William Curwen, who sold it to Councillor R.C. Penhale, president of the Old Folks Movement. Councillor Penhale (after whom the property is now named) gave the house and grounds to the local council to be used as an Old Folks Home. In the grounds at the present time is a pleasant little senior citizen's retirement estate.

The seaward end of Main Street was always an attraction to holiday-makers, especially at high tide, while at low tide the beach around the little shore café was a favourite gathering place. In the 1930s the interior of Greese House became Mrs Lund's Tea Rooms. In later years teas were served only in the garden.

As noted earlier the location of the village post office has changed several time over the years. In the 1920s it appears to have been located at Greese House (as indicated by the wall-plaque on the left) before the premises became Mrs Lund's Tea Rooms. The cart standing on its rear end by the beach can be seen in many other photographs from around this period.

Greese House cottages and gardens today.

A turbulent sea pounding over rocks is always a thrilling sight. Dogs especially enjoy it! But turbulent waves pounding inches away from the Beach Café was something other than exciting for the owner of these less-than-permanent structures. With a wind behind it, the tide could sweep up Main Street as far as Bailey Lane.

It's that cart again, this time parked beside the Royal Hotel stables. This postcard appears to give another indication of Heysham's reputation as a place where the sick might be restored to health. Cissie, who posted the card on 26 August 1929 to her friend Miss M. Wood of Heckmondwicke, wrote: 'Arrived here after all. Mother still keeping well, the weather is all one could wish.'

The wall-plaque at Cosy Corner declaring 'Mrs J. Kellett's Tea Rooms' shows how the tea room craze spread throughout the entire village, even to the smallest properties, while the reverse side of the card, posted on 2 August 1923, gives an indication of the type of relationship which existed between tradespeople and their regular customers in the these bygone days. The card is addressed to Mr Yates, Butcher of 9 Whalley Road, Clayton-le-Moors and asks simply: 'Dear Mr and Mrs Yates, Will you please save me a small fillet of lamb and oblige. Also will you kindly ask Mrs Rushton to save two cobs, Yours faithfully, Mrs Clark.'

At what period in Heysham's history, we wonder, did Cosy Corner slip down onto the foreshore?

More than ten years later, and there it is again! The owner of the cart allegedly left home with it every morning in an attempt to convince his wife that he was industriously engaged in some worthwhile activity. This postcard was sent in 1941 by a railway employee to his wife in Ealing, London, promising to be home next week for a night or two.

The same scene today, minus the cart, suggests that although the population of Greater Heysham has increased by a tremendous amount in recent years, as far as Heysham Village is concerned the stresses and strains of life in today's fast lane were designed to be enjoyed elsewhere.

This stately home was built in 1839 by Thomas Rawesthorne, a solicitor practising in Lancaster, to accommodate his large family. At the time Thomas and his wife Ann were owner-occupiers of the earlier Heysham Hall, now the Old Hall Inn. Thomas died on 27 November 1854 leaving ten children. Ann died on 26 March 1862.

These arches still exist. Roofless and leading nowhere, they appear to have some kind of religious connotation, although this could have been purely for effect. The Rawesthorne family grave can be found in St Peter's churchyard below St Patrick's chapel.

Heysham Hall was later occupied by the Hesketh family, and later still by the Graftons until the building of Heysham harbour began; then the property was used as a temporary hotel by the Midland Railway Company. Later the Hall was partly demolished and the stones used to build a row of cottages in Smithy Lane.

This part of the main building and the 'religious' archways are all that remain of the once palatial Heysham Hall. A sad reminder of days gone by.

There were several pumps and wells around the village before Morecambe Corporation began supplying Heysham with fresh water in 1909. Most were in back gardens of private properties. The two best-remembered public wells are St Patrick's Well near the church entrance in Main Street, and the Sainty Well between Carr Garth and Mary Street, now St Mary's Road. In this view of St Mary's Road the Sainty Well can be reached through the turn off on the right.

Today, looking down St Mary's Road towards Bailey Lane, what remains of the Sainty Well can be found in the back garden of one of the properties on the left.

Standing close to the village pump, the first watering-hole en route from the dock at Sunderland Point, was once a small coach house. Horses and passengers were rested and fed there in preparation for their journey across Morecambe Bay Sands. Sometime during the seventeenth century two cottages were built adjacent to the coach house; they were later converted into a single property with the coach house as kitchen. It is not known when the old Viking term for the area, Carr Garth, was first used, but in the early 1800s the property became Carr Garth School, with James Mashiter as schoolmaster. Many of the area's gentry are believed to have sent their children here to be educated, and based solely on the fact that 'J.W. 1854' is scratched on the kitchen window, one of the pupils is said to have been James Williamson, later Lord Ashton, best remembered today for his Lancaster park and monument. The Heysham Directory for 1851 claims that the school was 'built and supported by John Knowlys Esq. of Heysham Tower'. It appears that John Knowlys was regarded as having built the school as it was he who converted the two original cottages into a single property for this purpose. His reason for opening another school in opposition to the existing one, now St Peter's, was that although at the time St Peter's was a National School run by the Church of England, Mr Knowlys thought that it was not evangelical enough. During the First World War Carr Garth School was used as a convalescent home for officers, while other ranks convalesced at the old rectory. In 1920 the property was bought by the Church of England and used as a holiday home for the incumbents of poor parishes. Later it was resold and used for many years as a private guest house.

The construction of this fine old Elizabethan mansion house, known originally as Heysham Hall, and commonly called Wren Hall, began before 1580 but was not completed until 1598. The property was first occupied by Robert Edmondson, his son William and William Mashiter. The Edmondson's were once believed to have been the builders, although this is questionable. After the Edmondson family finally vacated the property in the late eighteenth century there were several owner-occupiers, the two most notable being Thomas Rawesthorne and Revd John Royds. It was during extensive restoration that John Royds discovered the priest hole which entered through the fireplace into a passage between the walls and exited several hundred yards along School Road. The property was eventually bought by William Mitchell Barker and opened as The Old Hall Inn in September 1958.

Before 1920 the Strawberry Gardens were literally strawberry gardens, where for a penny visitors could pick their own strawberries. In the grounds at the time were aviaries, conservatories, children's rides, greenhouses, a hotel and an early off-licence run by James Aldren. There was even a lawn tennis court. The complex, although not as well remembered as Heysham's later tourist attractions, was popular enough at the time for Morecambe's holiday-makers to be transported there by a horse-drawn tram service which terminated at the entrance.

Although the harbour had commenced operating in 1904 there were no public attractions beyond this point. Heysham's first golf course was situated opposite the Strawberry Gardens. Soon after the tram service had changed from horse-drawn to petrol-driven came the First World War. Because of the shortage of petrol the trams were then forced to operate on gas which was contained in huge canvas holders situated on top of the vehicles. When the war ended in 1918 the trams were converted back to petrol, but the austerity of the war years and their aftermath had seriously curtailed the tourist trade.

Heysham's first petrol-driven tram.

In 1920 the owners of the Strawberry Gardens, the Wyton family, sold the property to a development company. Soon the attractions and the now forgotten Strawberry Gardens tower had disappeared to make room for houses and shops. Only the hotel and vehicle park remained. These were purchased by Mr Walter Birtles of the Crown Hotel, Morecambe, under a separate agreement. After the death of Mr Birtles in 1949, his son sold the hotel to Messrs William Younger and Sons, in whose hands the property has remained until the present day.

The Strawberry Gardens Hotel today.

The treasurer of Heysham's first golf club was Mr R.B. Lee, a well-known grocer and provision merchant. The club house (above) was situated opposite Rayner's Old Heysham Café, which later became Heysham's first walk-round store owned by the Parker family. The store is best remembered as Costcutters, run after the retirement of Mr Parker by his two sons, Malcolm and John. The friendly atmosphere and personal service made the store immensely popular, but tragically John died several years ago and Malcolm has since retired. The premises are now owned by the Co-op.

Opposite: An advertisement for grocer and provision merchant R.B. Lee of Woborrow Road, *c.* 1920.

R. B. LEE

GROCER AND PROVISION MERCHANT,
HEYSHAM.

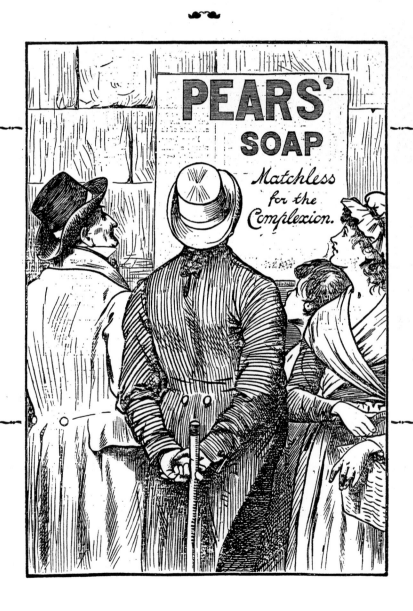

The Grosvenor Hotel on Sandylands promenade was once a fine hotel where non-residents could spend an evening dining and dancing. Many newly-married couples held their wedding receptions there, and many stars from the Morecambe shows stayed there as guests.

This imposing property at Higher Heysham has not yet been identified. The sender of this card claims that she is not so lonely this week as her husband is with her. Also she has only a short time to serve, and will be pleased to get back home.

Five
A Good Time was had by All

Winter fun on Heysham Barrows.

As early as 1820 when Heysham's residents were 'divided between a race of old yeomanry, tenants at rack rents and poor families earning a wretched subsistence by unskilled fishing', Heysham was fast becoming 'a place of fashionable resort for sea-bathing', according to Revd Thomas Dunham Whitaker, rector of Heysham 1813-19, in his *History of Richmondshire*. In the 1850s excursion trains began arriving in Morecambe, another popular sea-bathing resort, and for many years afterwards Heysham catered to the overflow from Morecambe's holiday trade. After being put firmly on the map in 1904 with the construction of the new harbour, Heysham became a holiday resort in its own right. Heysham Towers (Morecambe Bay) Holiday Camp opened in 1925, and a year later Septimus Wray of Ilkley bought the land known as Heysham Head. This he quickly turned into a highly popular family entertainment centre, and after that the fortunes of Heysham Village soared as visitors flocked in from both the holiday camp and the nearby resort of Morecambe.

Even in the days of Heysham Head and Morecambe Bay Holiday Camp, gentlemen on the beach, unless actually swimming, took their pleasure wearing shirts, slacks and sometimes jackets. Some daring young ladies might pose self-consciously in bathing costumes which never got wet, but as far as the men were concerned a bare chest on the beach would have had the same effect as Clark Gable's vest when he appeared on the screen wearing it!

In the halcyon days before sweatshirts and trainers, there was no need to display signs on the windows of restaurants informing customers that 'shoes and shirts must be worn'.

Harold, who may have worked at the holiday camp, appears to have had a little trouble. He posted this card on 15 August 1938: 'Dear Girls, I have just received parcel. Thanking you for same. The weather is quite nice today so I think I'll chance a dip. Was able to get another key from the camp here.'

Originally this building, which had a single tower, was known as Heysham Tower. The plural 'towers' came into popular use later as a tag for tourist hotels, holiday camps and other attractions, e.g. Alton Towers, Fawlty Towers etc. Heysham Tower, after its initial use as a gentleman's residence, became a hotel.

Before Heysham Tower and grounds opened as a holiday camp in 1925, the Tower building itself, to the confusion of later local historians, was known as the Midland Hotel. Even more confusingly postcards at the time were often inscribed 'The Midland Hotel, Morecambe'.

As a holiday camp, run by Mr and Mrs B.S. Holden, the Tower building was able to accommodate 400 guests. Later another 100, men only, were accommodated in tents in the grounds. Postcards sent from the camp by girls with such grand old names as Bessie, Lissie, Florrie and, grandest of all, Gertie, usually contained the same basic message: 'Lovely time... food excellent... weather marvellous.'

Mansion from conservatory lawn, Heysham Towers

Heysham Tower, standing in thirteen acres of private land surrounded by a high wall, was built in the early nineteenth century by J.T. Knowlys Esq. When the place became a holiday camp it was known alternatively as Heysham Towers or Morecambe Bay Holiday Camp. During the Second World War the premises were converted into a training camp for officer cadets, but quickly re-opened as a holiday camp after the war. In the immediate post-war years, with holidays abroad still a dream of the future, the camp became immensely popular.

HEYSHAM TOWER Camp and Guest House MORECAMBE

As a result of the declining fortunes of the British holiday industry Heysham Towers Holiday Camp eventually closed. The final blow was struck by the local council when the new owner was refused permission to situate a number of caravans in the grounds.

After being sold to a housing developer the Tower building was demolished and houses built on the site and in the grounds. The Tower Cottages, which stood on the edge of the grounds, are all that remain today.

Although converted into flats, the Tower Cottages even today present an imposing façade. Opposite the cottages is Heysham's amazingly picturesque main bus terminus. This fare-stage was officially designated 'Heysham Towers' by the bus company many years ago.

This archway was once the rear entrance to Heysham Tower, which for many years was the meeting place of 'John o' Gaunt's Bowmen'. There was a long-standing tradition at Heysham in relation to bows and arrows. Those used to such devastating effect by the Lonsdale Archers in the sixteenth century were manufactured at de Moleyne's mill just off Middleton Road.

Not a military photographer's shot of the D-Day landings, just a photograph of Heysham Sands in 1944, in the days before holiday-makers deserted the English coastal resorts. The writer of this card appears to have been another of the walking wounded: 'Been to Morecambe for the day. Plenty of people about. Just come from Heysham. Sat on a seat to write this. Am feeling much better again but the doctor is still visiting me.'

Two years earlier, in 1942, Harry from Barnoldswick had sent this card to his wife: 'Dear Lois, I am unable to get home this week-end. The boss came to us this afternoon and told us we had to work till 9 p.m. tonight, but another chap and I refused to do it. I was drenched to the skin and would not work any longer than 4 p.m. I spent last night with Mr and Mrs Hartley and had a warm supper.'

73

According to some, the entertainments at Heysham Head were cheap and tawdry, yet in spite of it everyone from six to sixty loved the place. Perhaps it was the rambling, shanty-town carelessness of it all. Although the walled gardens were lovingly cared for, the entertainments seemed to have been set up wherever and whenever an empty space could be found.

For kids a visit to Heysham Head with its rides, swings, marionette shows, parrots, monkeys, and even a circus, was a wild-eyed plunge into a magical world of breath-taking adventure, and the thrill of it all would linger in the memory forever, growing warmer and more poignant as the years went by.

In every corner of the grounds something was going on. Cheap and tawdry it may have been, yet stumbling on something that had not been there yesterday was an excitement beyond human understanding. Pinky and Perky performed at Heysham Head, as did Punch and Judy and Yorkshire Bob. Amongst the human entertainers there was a female clairvoyant, a female ventriloquist known as Windy Lyle, and Uncle Billy Mann who compèred the children's talent competitions and whistled 'If I were a blackbird'. For those who felt the occasional need to escape from it all there were many quiet corners where the weary and the thoughtful could find solace.

Poets' Corner, Heysham Head Old English Gardens.

Old English Gardens, Heysham Head.

Judging by these tranquil scenes it may be difficult to believe that close by was a circus, a slot-machine arcade with distorting mirrors, open-air dancing, a screeching peacock, a daily concert party, brass bands on Sunday, and Uncle Billy Mann still whistling 'If I were a blackbird'. Miss Pugh sent his brief note to a friend in Yorkshire on 13 July 1837: 'Dear friend, Just a line. We were here this morning. Hundreds of roses. Girls coming tomorrow.'

With the date stamped on their wrists in purple dye, visitors to Heysham Head who tired of the swings and roundabouts, marionette shows, concert parties and Uncle Billy Mann's whistling, could leave by the main entrance for a stroll around the village, or through the beach doorway for a romp on the rocks, and return later.

This view of the rocks beneath Heysham Head's beach doorway dates from times when political correctness was an MP standing up for the national anthem. Annie, who sent this postcard to her friend Edna in Yorkshire wrote: 'Dear Edna, What do you think of the weather now? Isn't it favouring us? We are like three little darkies. We are seriously considering starting a nigger minstrel troupe on the sands to make expenses to stay another week. Funds are getting low, so if you have 'owt' to spare send it to me at once, Annie.'

The Great House on Heysham Head was built by George Wright (around 1816) who had previously been steward to John Marsden of Hornby Castle. In yet another attempt to confound future historians the house was originally named The Barrows and later Heysham Lodge. Later still it was often referred to as The Hall, not to be confused with Heysham Hall or The Old Hall, and sometimes The Manor House, although it was never a manor house.

The Great House later became part amusement arcade, part café, and part residence. The entrance fee to Heysham Head was sixpence. Everything else was free, apart from refreshments. In later years a miniature train carried visitors from the forecourt up the steep driveway onto the Head.

Around the front of the Great House were chairs and benches where adults could relax in the sun while the kids ran safe and free. Inside Gandy's circus-tent the tumblers tumbled and the tight-rope walkers walked their tight-ropes, while in the Rose Garden Uncle Billy Mann went on whistling and a boy with an angelic voice and a calliper on his leg sang *Jerusalem*. Later in the day the Concert Party arrived to sing and dance and play their accordions – and all for sixpence! Most visitors swore that there was nowhere else in the country quite like Heysham Head – and there never will be again.

ROSE GARDENS, HEYSHAM HEAD.

The Rocks, Heysham.

Unlike the men of a few years later who wore shirts and slacks on the beach, in 1914 men of a certain standing wore suits – and the ladies – well, no wonder the gentleman in the Homburg hat is watching so intently!

HIGH TIDE, HEYSHAM.

G5028.

Once again the excitement mounts around the beach café as the tide approaches. This is certainly not a scene from *Baywatch*, and all the better for it. On this beach there are no muscle-bound macho-men 'pumping iron' – and when you've seen one Pamela Anderson you've seen 'em all – so they say!

These two postcards both show scenes of Half Moon Bay, with one of the harbour breakwaters at one end and Heysham Head's beach doorway at the other. Although the wearing of shirts on the beach may have been compulsory, the wearing of braces, one would imagine, was optional. On some beaches rows of permanent bathing huts were erected by the local council and could be hired by the day or the week. These shown here were privately owned and were carried to the beach by men whose wives preferred not to disrobe under the watchful gaze of gentlemen in Homburg hats. 'We are having a good time and lovely weather', claimed Kath on 21 August 1935, 'This is where we have done most of our bathing.'

In 1928 Morecambe and Heysham were amalgamated. One year later the remaining bone of contention, Heysham's independently-owned foreshore from the Battery to Half Moon Bay, was sold by the proprietors of the manor to Morecambe Corporation for £800. Fishing rights had been relinquished some time ago as the result of a drawn-out legal battle with a Morecambe fisherman.

The Sunny Slopes, one of Heysham's more genteel attractions, still exist. The gently winding pathways and stone stairways, and the carefully designed outcroppings of rock, have changed little over the years. The deck chairs have gone of course, and the holiday-makers have long since jetted off into a foreign sunset, but the unrestricted view across Morecambe Bay and the vast panorama of sea and sky remain to be marvelled at by any one who can find the time to stand and stare.

In the days before cyclists of all ages realized they could break the law with impunity, the only cyclist seen in this photograph is observing the 'no cycling' signs and pushing his bicycle, while pedestrians stroll in safety along Sandylands promenade. The spring which fed the little boating pool has since mysteriously disappeared and the pool is now dry.

This fishing and boating pool hopefully will never dry. Even on the grimmest of days, whether fishing in the bay or from the promenade, the hills across Morecambe Bay provide an impressive backdrop to this kind of sea-side activity.

Six
St Peter's Church

To the delight of both visitors and locals, all that ever changes in Heysham Village are the seasons.

This ancient church, the beginnings of which date from around AD 700, was officially registered as a place of Christian worship in AD 967, almost one hundred years before the Norman Conquest of Britain. The Millennium celebrations staged at Heysham in 1967 extended throughout the summer and attracted many Christian dignitaries, including the Archbishops of York and Dublin.

Old Porch, Heysham Church . 1030

Unbelievably, this early monument to the establishment of Christianity in Britain has been allowed to fall into disrepair. Many fund-raising events have been staged in recent years in an attempt to save the church from closure.

Benches have been donated in the past for use by anyone wishing to linger in the serenity of St Peter's churchyard, but beware! Amongst those trees there exists a time warp! Enter it and within minutes an hour will have passed. For those with urgent business to attend to later in the day, to sit on a bench could be a disaster. Close your eyes for a moment and the time-shifters will creep in without warning and steal the hours away!

One of St Peter's grey squirrels stops its scurrying for a moment to pose for the camera, while from another corner of the churchyard the Grosvenor Hotel can be seen standing against Heysham's familiar backdrop of sea and sky.

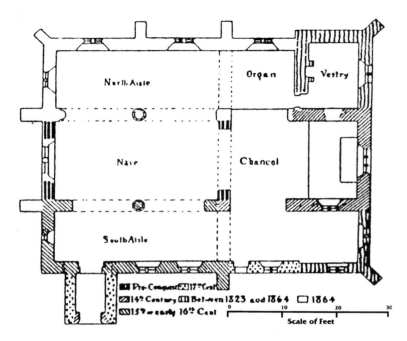

PLAN OF HEYSHAM CHURCH

As evident from this plan very little of the pre-Conquest stonework still exists. The porch is seventeenth century, while surrounding it is mostly earlier fifteenth or sixteenth-century stonework.

And finally here he is, the man himself, still as industriously employed as ever, trying to decide whether to sit in the churchyard for a while, or adjourn to the Royal Hotel for a pint or two of the landlord's very best bitter beer!

Seven

The Harbour

Heysham Harbour's Sealink service, terminated in the 1970s.

According to Midland Railway Co., paper No. 3635, towards the end of 1891 Mr James Abernathy was consulted as to the construction of a dock at Heysham, in Morecambe Bay, in connection with their railway system. The Midland Railway had for years experienced difficulty, and were incurring considerable expense in maintaining their existing pier and harbour accommodation at Morecambe, where it was only possible for steamers and vessels to enter and leave the harbour near the period of high water; moreover the channel leading to Morecambe was difficult to navigate. Mr Abernethy was impressed with the natural advantages which the proposed site afforded, as being in close proximity to Heysham Lake, a deep-water channel having a depth of forty feet at low-water of ordinary spring tides. In 1896 the Midland Railway Company obtained an Act for the construction of the harbour but in March of that year Mr James Abernethy died. Mr George Neill Abernethy was then appointed joint chief engineer with Mr J. Allen MacDonald. The preparation of the detailed plans was at once commenced, and in July 1897 the contract was put out to tender and was let to Messrs Price and Wills of Westminster.

In addition to the Joint Chief Engineers, Mr J. Allen MacDonald and Mr George Neill Abernethy, the Resident Engineer at the commencement of the work was Mr Gerald Fitzgibbon who left in September 1899, and Mr Baldwin H. Bent, who replaced him and remained until completion.

'London to Londonderry or the Giant's Causeway, the whole journey performed over the property of one railway only, once a dream is now a reality.' (From an article by W.F. Nokes in *The Railway Magazine*)

'That mammoth of enterprise, the Midland Railway, being in possession of the cream of the holiday and tourist traffic from the districts from which it takes its name, needed one link to complete its chain of communication... A bridge was impossible, a tunnel beneath the Irish Sea impracticable, so, with its characteristic acumen, the railway built a fleet of well-equipped steamers to navigate the intervening distance.' (W.F. Nokes)

. New Dock at Heysham.

'The possibility of further development in the Heysham district may be somewhat retarded until the landowners realize their possessions are not quite equal to Hampstead, Kensington, or other popular centres. Until the symptoms of the disease of inflammation of the unearned increment have subsided no capitalist will come along to build. This is to be regretted, as it is quite conceivable that the land contiguous to the northern breakwater might eventually become a holiday resort.' (W.F. Nokes)

HEYSHAM HARBOUR FROM THE LIGHTHOUSE. 1220

L.M.S. Heysham Camp. 90990.

The future holiday resort mentioned by W.F. Nokes referred to a scheme proposed by the Midland Railway and put into practice by the London Midland and Scottish Railway (LMS). Excursion trains brought holiday makers to Heysham Harbour where they spent a week or two in one of the Company's Camping Coaches (called caravans in a 1911 brochure) along the Middleton Sands side of the above-mentioned northern breakwater.

L.M.S. Camping Coach, Heysham. 9098

Following the closure of its traditional route in 1966 the Leeds boat train ran via Carnforth to Morecambe. Other through services continued until Heysham lost its Irish passenger sailings. After that, with just the Isle of Man passenger ferries remaining, only the London train ran through to Heysham. The boat train service ceased in 1974.

Rail services to and from Heysham ceased completely as soon as the closure formalities for the four mile section between Morecambe and Heysham were completed. However, an infrequent service recommenced in the 1990s.

Eight

Heysham
Yesterday and Today

A twelfth-century Crusader welcomes twenty-first-century visitors to Heysham's eighth-century church.

There must be very little to do at Heysham these days, it has been said, with no Heysham Head and no holiday camp patrons for local businesses to cater to. Simple pleasures like swimming at Half Moon Bay or strolling along the vastness of Heysham Sands are out of fashion, Gandy's Circus has long-since rolled up its big top for the last time, the parrots, monkeys and distorting mirrors are gone, the peacock has stopped its screeching and Uncle Billy Mann no longer whistles 'If I were a blackbird'. So apart from eating and drinking in the pubs and cafés around the village, what else is there to do? Nothing perhaps for today's wizard of the computer keyboard, but for many others Heysham is still a vast treasure trove of delight. In addition to the ever-present reminders of Heysham's ancient past, anyone who catches one of the weekend celebrations will find themselves transported back in time, back to those eager, fun-filled days of not-so-long-ago. Here a parade marches past, over there is a jazz band or an open-air brass band concert. Market stalls line the little main street and spill over onto the village green, and through it all strides a twelfth-century knight. On less spectacular occasions you can doze away a lazy afternoon half-watching a local cricket match, or do a little browsing around the phenomenon of modern times, the giant car boot sale. On weekdays when there are no festivals, car boot sales or vintage car rallies, steam rallies or gymkhana, get out your camera and binoculars or simply sit and marvel at the creations of man and nature!

The entrance to the cliff footpath also gave access to Salem Farm. The gentleman seen here is believed to be Robert Swindlehurst, the owner of the farm. The public right of way originally ran along the foreshore, but this could only be used when the tide allowed. A more elevated route was needed, so Mr Swindlehurst allowed the seaward edge of his property to be used. The postcard below, date stamped 1911, shows the footpath running precariously along the cliff edge after the rest of the farm had been fenced off from the public.

After the building of the promenade the footpath was no longer needed, but although still precarious, the public seemed to prefer it. Later the promenade was widened and the cliff face banked up, making the footpath safe both day and night.

The Cliff Footpath , Heysham

Ho-hum! The same boringly idyllic scene viewed from the same vantage point. Today's photograph must be even more boringly idyllic than yesterday's postcard to anyone who enjoys the bustling, fume-filled, traffic-jammed excitement of a city street. And why has no developer come along in all these years to build a row of nice houses overlooking the sea?

The writer of this card, posted in October 1908, claimed: 'We walked to this place from Morecambe yesterday. It is lovely country round here. You would like it. Just like Wales.' Does this mean that Wales is, or was, just like Morecambe Bay? Lucky people the Welsh! Would the writer recognize this place today, now that the gas lamp has been replaced by an electric light?

Heysham Rectory

As the rector of the day was regarded as 'lord of the manor of Lower Heysham' the entrance to the church and rectory is known as Manor Court Yard. In the days of the old rectory there was no through road to Chapel Hill and the Barrows as there is today. As indicated in the postcard above, beyond the gates was rectory land. The route used by locals was through the churchyard and up the embankment between the ancient stone walls. Visitors who were unaware of this took the beach route over the rocks and around the point.

Manor Court Yard today.

Car boot sales and rallies are regularly held here on the village green, yet when the vehicles and the hundreds of pairs of trampling feet have returned home the grass seems to spring back to life again fresher and cleaner that it looks in the postcard above.

A perfect spot for a village car boot sale, right next to the village car park. In the photograph below, the litter has been removed, the churned-up mud has dried and an air of orderly calm has settled over the village green once again.

Even to non-cricket fans, there is nothing more relaxing on a gentle sunny afternoon than the sound of leather on willow. Other sounds can also be relaxing in their own way. When the little ensemble below starts to play, people have been known to drift into a semi-hypnotic state while relaxing to the soothing tone of the cornet, clarinet and big trombone, fiddle, cello, big bass drum, bassoon, flute and euphonium!

Meanwhile, in other parts of Heysham, life goes on at its usual tranquil pace. Who cares if the sea gets angry or the rush-hour traffic becomes congested once in a while? On the other hand if the Queen and Prince Philip should happen to drive by, as below, the whole place erupts with excitement.

Early nineteenth century records state that in the whole of Heysham there were no more than 110 dwellings occupied by 106 families, a total of 540 persons, and ninety-three of these families were employed in agriculture. Of the others nine were in trade and four in professional pursuit or unemployed. The last two pursuits appear to be have been rated equally. Judging by these two views of Heysham Village in the early 1900s the population appears to have increased very little. The gentleman in the bottom photograph is once again believed to be Robert Swindlehurst, owner of Salem Farm.

Today in Heysham there are doctors, lawyers, business executives, office workers, shop assistants, and those who stand on street corners with mobile telephones glued to their ears – but very few farming families! Luckily the few who still exist appear not to suffer from 'the disease of inflammation of the unearned increment' (W.F. Nokes), and have so far resisted the advances of the rampant developer, as indicated by these unrestricted views of distant hills across open meadow and pasture land.

The terraced properties seen here are now part of Knowlys Road. When the photograph for this postcard was taken this was Woborrow Terrace, before the bungalows in Knowlys Road were built. Knowlys Road ended at No. 26. Since then the ivy-covered cottage on St Mary's Road has been uncovered and the village pump has gone. It was destroyed in the dark by a motor vehicle in 1930. Now the area has street lighting and the road has been laid.

The Rocks Heysham
Morecambe Bay Holiday Camp. Heysham Towers

PHOTO BY
W. HORNER

Although these photographs of Throbshaw Point and Lion's Head were taken eighty years apart they are uncannily similar, even down to the positioning of the boat sailing past. The rocks seen in the recent photograph were deposited by the local council to prevent further erosion of the cliff face. Throbshaw Point, of course, had nothing whatsoever to do with the holiday camp at Heysham Towers.

When the sea becomes agitated it has a magnetic attraction. It also has a mind to go where it wants, and heaven help anything that stands in its way. The photograph above gives an indication of what became of the old Pot House Café, pictured below.

Nine

Heysham Heritage Association

Historic Chapel Hill, now owned and protected by the National Trust.

Joseph Mallord William Turner, one of the greatest of British artists, noted for capturing the expression of light, atmosphere and mood of the elements in his paintings, had first visited the Lancaster area in 1797 after crossing Morecambe sands by coach from Ulverston. He was so impressed with the breathtaking views across Morecambe Bay that he returned in 1816. On 8 August 1816 he visited Heysham where he made several sketches from which he later produced such works as 'Heysham and Cumberland Mountains' (copyright The British Museum) above, which depicts Heysham Village, the coastal landscape to the north of the village, the sea and the Cumberland fells beyond. This vista is still greatly enjoyed and valued by residents and visitors. Several other well-known watercolours painted by Turner of scenes in the Lancaster area are published by Lancaster City Council as a series of quality greeting cards. In 1996 Heysham Heritage Association funded the addition of the watercolour above to this series of cards. It holds a very special place in the history of the Association.

This postcard of the coastal fields to the north of Heysham village, viewed from Knowlys Road, dates from the mid-twentieth century. The atmosphere is pastoral and scenic and is similar to parts of the Turner landscape. When a planning application for housing on a small part of this coastal land was submitted in January 1990, over 200 copies of a handwritten circular opposing the proposal were distributed by Barbara and Ron Verhoef; letters and petitions were submitted to Lancaster City Council. In 1991 a much more substantial planning application was submitted for nearly eighty houses covering the majority of this landscape. This inexorably threatened the famous Turner vista, so the Association assembled a petition against the application with nearly 1,000 signatures. Many other letters were written and a public meeting organized by the local Neighbourhood Council. The application was considered simultaneously with a Public Local Plan Inquiry and rejected by the Inspector from the Department of the Environment.

Heritage
HEYSHAM
Association

Mesolithic
Scraper

At a meeting in August 1990 of residents keen to conserve the coastal landscape, those in attendance decided to call themselves 'Heysham Heritage Association'. But more importantly those present decided to continue working together whatever the outcome of the planning applications. They also agreed to adopt concern for other open coastal fields around Heysham and for Heysham Head. The Association, with Barbara Verhoef as its secretary, was now on the way to being firmly established. The Association then decided to make positive steps towards conserving the heritage of Heysham. Two significant ideas were proposed, one for a heritage centre in Heysham village, and the other to try to involve the National Trust in protecting the coastal land. In November 1992 a proposal for a centre was sent to Lancaster City Council's Director of Development. The following year a more detailed proposal was submitted to the Neighbourhood Council and received unanimous support. Other heritage centres were visited and as a result the Association was able to involve the Heritage Trust for the North West, based at Pendle Heritage Centre, to help achieve their goal.

Pendle Heritage Centre

Early in 1993 an invitation was sent the National Trust to view the Barrows Field on Heysham Head. This was Diocesan land, leased to Lancaster City Council until 1996 for public access. After that its future was uncertain. The Regional Director, Oliver Maurice, was shown round the Barrows Field, the ancient monument of St Patrick's chapel and the rock graves by the rector, Revd Eric Lacey, and members of the Association. After appropriate fundraising the Trust were able to purchase the land in 1996 as part of their Enterprise Neptune scheme. The previous year (1995) Lancaster City Council set up the Heysham Regeneration Project at a meeting of the Economic Development Committee addressed by the Director of the Heritage Trust for the North West, John Miller. To house Heysham's proposed new heritage centre several properties were considered, funds raised from architectural bodies, and eventually a centre was opened in April 2000.

The Association organized events to raise awareness of the heritage among local people and to raise funds for its projects. Since J.M.W. Turner is identified as a key figure in Heysham's more recent history, a Turner Week was held in the summer of 1996 with the help of Lancaster Arts and Events. This featured an Artist in Residence working in local primary schools, an art exhibition, guided walks, residents wearing Georgian dress and a Georgian Fayre at the Royal Hotel. Pictured left, displaying the special Georgian Fayre menu are (left to right), Gary Standen, then landlord of the Royal Hotel; local artist Rod Hargreaves and chairman of Heysham Heritage Association John Holding.

Mayor Councillor Janet Horner (left) presenting prizes at St Peter's School hall to the winners of the Turner Week art competition. From left to right are Malcolm Haynes, Elizabeth Jeffs, Irene Morris and Heather Satterley. (Photograph from *The Visitor*).

Under the guidance of Lancaster City Council's Director of Development Charles Wilson, some of the funding for the centre was provided by the Coast Heritage Project, a European Union initiative designed to connect heritage projects in different countries. Exchange 'networking' visits were arranged as part of the project, so that each could learn from each other. Gathered outside St Peter's church in December 1997 (right) are the rector, Revd Eric Lacey, the deputy mayor, Margaret Rainford, representatives from Corsica and Killough (in Northern Ireland), together with members of the Association, the Neighbourhood Council, the National Trust, Lancaster City Council and Council Officers. (Photograph from *The Visitor*)

Under the guidance of John Miller, Director of the Heritage Trust for the North West, further sources of funding were found. Early in 1998 two empty shops in a grade 2 listed building, previously a barn, in Heysham's Main Street were acquired. Stephen Gardner, architect for Lancaster City Council, was commissioned to draw up plans for converting the building into a heritage centre. In April 2000 the centre was opened to the public by Dr Anthony Leeming (centre left), chairman of the National Trust North West Region. Also present are the mayor and mayoress (centre right), Stephen Gardner (extreme right) and John Holding (extreme left), the chairman of the Association.

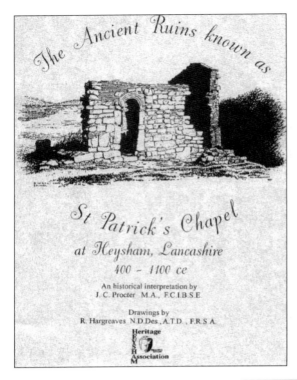

The Ancient Ruins known as

St Patrick's Chapel

at Heysham, Lancashire

400 – 1100 ce

An historical interpretation by
J. C. Procter M.A., F.C.I.B.S.E.

Drawings by
R. Hargreaves N.D.Des., A.T.D., F.R.S.A.

Heritage
Association

In 1997 there was an ecumenical Celtic Pilgrimage from Rome to Derry, Northern Ireland, commemorating 1,400 years since St Augustine came to England from Rome, and since the death of St Columba. The pilgrimage passed through Heysham in June and there was a very well attended open-air service at St Peter's Church. To coincide with this event the Association published a short monograph about St Patrick's Chapel, written by John Procter, one of the first members of the Association, and illustrated by Rod Hargreaves.

Revd Eric Lacey, the rector of St Peter's from 1988 to 1998, was an enthusiastic and influential member of the Association from its early days. In 1991 he addressed a meeting of the Association about the history of the Village and church and later chaired several important meetings. With the approach of the new Millennium a national scheme for planting yew trees in churchyards was inaugurated by David Bellamy. The Association presented St Peter's Church church with a yew tree which was planted early in 1999 by Revd Eric Lacey (pictured here with spade) and Revd David Tickner, the new Rector from late in 1998.

It has been a policy of the National Trust for some years to protect the coastline from development. The organization started in the late nineteenth century in the Lake District, to protect the shores of Derwent Water from development. It was not surprising therefore that they seized on the opportunity in 1996 to protect the historic Heysham coast for present and future generations to enjoy.

Negotiations for the purchase of the Barrows Field and St Patrick's Chapel from the Diocese of Blackburn had started in 1993. In the spring of 1995, the centenary year of the Trust, the North West Director of the Trust, Oliver Maurice, completed a sponsored walk (the 'slog') along the coasts of Cumbria and Lancashire to raise funds for the purchase. He is pictured above (centre) on the rock graves at Heysham with Revd Eric Lacey, and some of his Trust colleagues who walked with him.

On the same spot in 1996 (the rock graves adjacent to St Patrick's Chapel) the official hand-over ceremony occurred at the same place. The Bishop of Blackburn, Rt Revd Alan Chesters, is pictured here handing over the purchase contract to Peter Sharp, chairman of the National Trust North West Region, together with Oliver Maurice. (Photograph from *The Visitor*)

In order to find their way around, visitors to Heysham need some form of introduction. With this in mind an eight-page 'trail' leaflet has been compiled and can be obtained from the Heritage Centre. This conducts visitors on a guided tour of the village including St Peter's Church and historic buildings such as Greese Cottage and Carr Garth. It also visits the supposed site from which J.M.W. Turner made his sketches in 1816. Engravings by Turner were used to illustrate *A History of Richmondshire*, a work compiled by the celebrated antiquarian Revd Thomas Dunham Whitaker, rector of Heysham from 1813 to 1819.

Another Heysham historian of the nineteenth century was Monsignor Gradwell, much quoted by twentieth-century local historian Dr F. Whewell Hogarth, and the Association has carried on this tradition of local histories. Eileen Dent had already written a short history of Heysham in 1993 (published by the Parochial Church Council at St Peter's) before she joined the Association. She followed this up in 1997 with a companion volume, *Voices of Heysham*. With the advent of the new Millennium Eileen was asked to compile another book, not just on Heysham this time, but on the entire peninsula of which Heysham is a part. Many members contributed chapters to this new book, which was published in 2000.

The HEYSHAM
PENINSULA

Edited by
Eileen J Dent

A collection of vivid vignettes of one of those hidden corners of England

Published by Heysham Heritage Association

The HISTORY
of HEYSHAM

A wide-angled view

by

David Flaxington

Sufficient funds to cover the printing costs for *The Heysham Peninsula* were obtained from the Millennium 'Awards For All' scheme, and with the typesetting being done locally by another Association member, this saving opened the way for a companion volume. It had been known for some time that David Flaxington had already compiled a history of Heysham, setting it in the wider context of the history of Britain. The Association was delighted when he agreed to adapt his work to the specification required by the funds available and the book was published in 2001. Rod Hargreaves designed the covers for both books.

The Story of HEYSHAM COAST

Another 'trail' leaflet published by the National Trust takes the visitor via St Patrick's Chapel and the rock-cut graves to the grand scenery of Heysham coast with its history and special wildlife. It also gives details of the Heysham Head Pleasure Gardens which were a dominant influence on Heysham in the mid-twentieth century. Both this and the *Heysham Village Trail* leaflet were designed by John Westwell of the Heritage Trust for the North West, who is also responsible for the design of the superb historical displays in the Heritage Centre, produced after careful and frequent consultations with local residents.

To the delight of both visitors and local enthusiasts, Heysham boasts a wildlife as well as a historical heritage. In the early spring the colour and richness of the flora is a sight to behold; the Barrows Field and the Rectory Wood are carpeted with bluebells, while the headstones and ancient crosses in St Peter's churchyard rise majestically out of a thick bed of crocuses. Less common plants and ferns can also be found in the churchyard and on the cliffs. In the spring and autumn many birds, some quite rare, migrate along the coastal land and through the bay; in winter, as the tide rises, flocks of wading birds appear as huge shadows over the surface of the water.

One of Heysham's most recent celebrations was held on the occasion of Her Majesty the Queen's Golden Jubilee. Heysham Heritage Centre is now an integral part of the village and to mark the occasion a special exhibition of life in Heysham in the 1950s, the decade of the Queen's Coronation, was mounted in the Centre. On this and similar occasions, the Association mounts a stall along with the others to raise funds for either the upkeep of the Centre or other local charitable purposes.

CLASSIC
WARBIRDS

CLASSIC

WARBIRDS

David Stubbs

OSPREY
AEROSPACE

Acknowledgements

So that a companion volume won't be required to thank everyone who helped, my thanks go to those mentioned throughout this book. They gave freely of their time; supplying information, insight and introductions. Not found in these pages but as deserving are Sara Hanna and Roger Hoefling. My thanks to you all.

For Pat, who was and will be there.

Published in 1991 by Osprey Publishing Limited
59 Grosvenor Street, London W1X 9DA

© David Stubbs

British Library Cataloguing in Publication Data

Stubbs, David
    Classic warbirds.
    623.746

ISBN 1855321750

Editor Dennis Baldry
Page design Paul Kime
Printed in Hong Kong

Front cover Between 1943 and 1945, the English region of East Anglia was an unsinkable aircraft carrier for the bombers and fighters of the US Eighth Air Force. This B-17G was one of six Flying Fortresses which helped to re-enact the reality of a daylight bombing mission over Nazi Germany in David Puttnam's 1990 motion picture, *Memphis Belle*

Back cover An extremely advanced and costly warplane in its day, the Lockheed P-38 Lightning was produced in response to a 1937 US Army Air Corps specification for a long-range interceptor (pursuit) and escort fighter. Lefty Gardner's pristine P-38 is one of only a handful of airworthy examples which have survived from a production run of 9942 aircraft

Title page Hawker Sea Fury at the Reno air races getting its skin waxed and canopy polished. Slippery is a good quality for an aeroplane in a hurry and you'd better be able to see clearly when you get there

Right David Stubbs is a commercial and editorial photographer specializing in aviation subjects. A pilot himself, this allows him to combine his interest in aircraft with his profession. His photographs appear in numerous magazines and trade journals and his subjects range from antiques to fly-by-wire aircraft. Now living in London, this transplanted Californian enjoys witnessing the affection shown by the British for aircraft—especially warbirds. This is his first book, and producing it allowed him to experience another facet of the business of flying

For a catalogue of all books published by Osprey Aerospace please write to:

**The Marketing Department,
Octopus Illustrated Books, 1st Floor, Michelin House,
81 Fulham Road, London SW3 6RB**

Introduction

While writing this book, people asked me a lot of questions. What kinds of aeroplanes is it about? Is it a historical book? How do you know what to write?

The answer to the last question was the easiest and also explains how this book was produced. Mostly, I collected answers to questions I had about warbirds. The information comes from warbird pilots; I just strung it together.

I grew up air-minded but am far from expert on the subject of aviation. The best way to locate experts is to publish a book and wait for the flood of letters outlining what was left out and/or wrong.

Of course I've left things out; perhaps some of your favourite things. They wouldn't all fit in. This is not an encyclopedia, a comprehensive history or a learn-to-fly book.

It's a 'what it feels like, looks like and sounds like' book. In these pages, I want to take you along to kick a few tyres, hear some lore and go flying.

David Stubbs
London
April 1991

Right Never mind the sun; the bright paint and polished aluminium are enough to make you need sunglasses. The reflection is of a North American P-51D Mustang *Huntress III* on a clear Nevada day

Contents

Fam Hop

The best way to see what warbirds are all about is through the windshield of one in flight. We'll be getting that view with an introductory flight (Fam Hop) in a North American T-6.

The T-6, also called the Texan or Harvard, was the highest performance single-engine trainer flown by most Allied aviation cadets before moving up to something operational. For some, it was the last type flown before finding another line of work altogether.

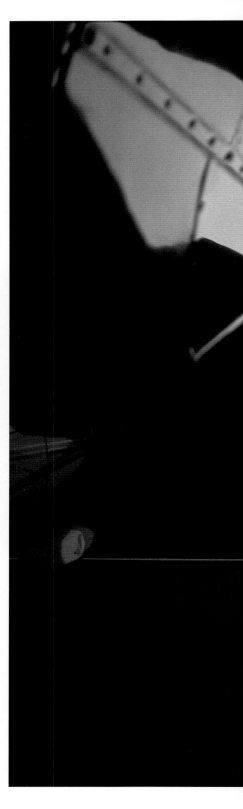

Right Six a.m. Usually, if your eyes are open at all, you're rubbing sleep from them. Not today. You're going flying in Gordon Kibby's T-6. His machine is hangared at the county airport at Livermore, California, 30 miles east of San Francisco. The sun comes up as the hangar door gets pushed open. Even under protective covers, N29GK looks ready to go

Above Without a proper tug, Gordon just has to make do. A wire-rope towing bridle attaches to the main gear. Your job is to walk the tail out and keep it going straight ahead. 'Just push on the rudder to steer; you can't hurt anything', says Gordon. No delicate assembly protected by 'No Push' stencils here. This is a two-handed machine built to withstand less than elegant handling

Right Some 7000 hours of work spread over seven years. Gordon says in the beginning it was 'Me, the credit union and $3000. I started with the fuselage and as I could afford parts, I got them'. It's worth close to $200,000 today. The project was completed in 1984 and he's put about 350 flying hours on the clock in the six years since

Above The covers come off revealing what seems like several acres of polished aluminium. Not exactly a low maintenance surface but who's going to admire a teflon aeroplane?

Why a T-6? Only so many pages in this book and we're going to squander some of them on anything less than a Mustang or a Spitfire? Well, yes and no. Combat aircraft clearly have the biggest fan clubs but nobody stepped into one straight off the street or farm.

The T-6 is a great choice for a fam hop. In a way, that's what it was built for. There were many schemes for military pilot training before and during World War 2. Something they had in common was that cadets started training on simple aircraft. A dwindling number advanced through the course with aircraft performance and complexity increasing in stages. The T-6 was the introduction to that level of complexity.

Many cadets' first flights were in light aircraft of civil lineage. Two-place Pipers and Aeroncas, weighing around 700 pounds empty traded hats and became military trainers.

Above Preflighting the aeroplane, you crouch down to sample some fuel. It's said about pilots with tail-dragger time that they pay more attention to the belly of an aeroplane than tricycle-only pilots do. Looking at an aeroplane's belly is like checking a thoroughbred's mouth; certain internal problems can be observed from without

Above right The wings are packed with things to check. Landing gear, tyres, brakes, flaps, ailerons and more on the list. With all the bells and whistles to remember, the wing itself shouldn't be overlooked. The leading edge should be free of big dents, dirt, ice and too many squashed bugs

Below right Ripples in the skin are signs of structural damage beneath. The polished surface makes them easy to spot

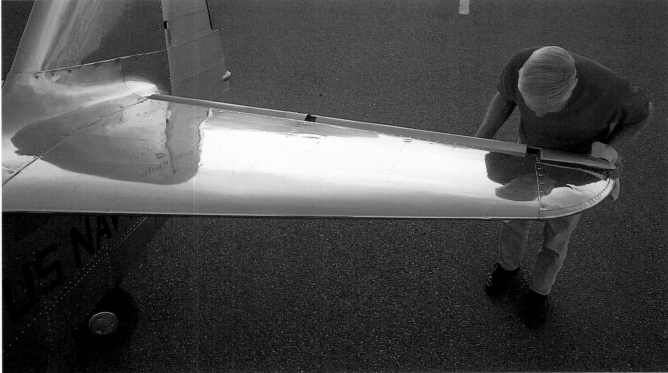

Above Up on the wing, checking the oil. Capacity is 10 US gallons and the engine will burn 1 pint to 1 quart per hour. The step up to the wing is a bit of a stretch but the 80 grit non-skid wing walk assures good footing. The wing feels very solid under foot. There are two ways to enable a structure to withstand stress. It can allow stress to pass through or it can stand firm. In other words, it can bend like a reed or stand like a proverbial masonry convenience

Right Time to mount up. It's best to arrange things in the cockpit before you get in and find yourself in the way. Unfasten the harness and lay the straps open, step right onto the seat, then settle into it. Headset cords make lousy stirrups when easing oneself into the saddle, so make sure to get yours out of the way

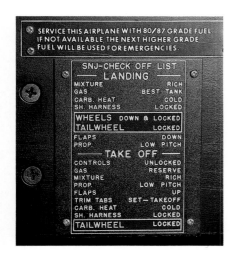

Opposite Fastening the harness presents you with a mild test on the order of matching pegs and holes of corresponding shapes. Held in by a seat belt and two shoulder belts, you feel joined to the seat. It's not so much that you're not going anywhere, but that the aeroplane isn't going anywhere without you. You get the feeling as you settle in and look around that a sizeable chunk of the aeroplane is in your lap. The panel is big and fills most of your forward view. The rest is taken up by the engine and its cowling. Tail down means engine up

Left The biggest lettering pertains to wheels. Failure to comply will assure the most trouble the soonest

Below A warbird's most vital piece of equipment. Some rebuild projects start with the builder's plate as the only recognizable bit of hardware in the pile

CLEAR! The Pratt & Whitney AN-1340 catches quickly, turning the propeller into a blur and the morning's calm into history. The engine's model number refers to its displacement in cubic inches. That's $22\frac{1}{3}$ litres. Rated at 600 hp, the engine is producing less than $\frac{1}{2}$ hp per inch of displacement. The low stage of tune under-taxes the engine and allows it to hum along happily while more mythical in-line powerplants are more prone to trouble. As a Mustang owner put it, 'Those radial engine guys keep going because they're not powered by hot water toilets'

Flying one of these classic aircraft today is a joy to be sure, but not that far removed from contemporary light aircraft flying. Anyway, because the ride is not that exotic, it won't do for a warbird fam hop.

Aircraft such as Stearman biplanes tested the cadets more fully with greater weight, speed and power. Today, these aircraft are popularly thought of as barnstormers. Since biplanes accounted for the great bulk of flying circus machines, it's an easy association to make.

A flight in a classic biplane is one of those change-your-life experiences. Open cockpit, big round motor and two rag wings with lots of wires and a dragging tail. Heaven. In fact, it's the nice part of Heaven.

As nice as all that is, it's not quite what we're looking for. For a warbird fam hop, you need an aircraft that looks and feels the part. You want something that won't require too much imagination to see yourself as Pappy Boyington's wingman for a while. But enough thinking and daydreaming; it's time to go flying.

Left S-turns during taxi keeps you at least intermittently in touch with your path ahead

Above Throttle up, brakes off. The take off roll is brief. The tail comes up in six seconds and the aeroplane breaks ground four seconds later. Climb out is at 120 mph

21

Left The panel tells the story. The view improves in level flight although from the back seat it's still restricted forward. With the engine running, the intercom isn't necessary for talking but it makes hearing a whole lot easier. As in possible

Below On the wing. An aeroplane does or doesn't fly by the graces of pressure created by air moving over its surfaces. If the leading edge lacks a correct profile, the wing won't work properly or at all. Not working properly means the wing may get you aloft in a nice straight line as you take off but lack sufficient lifting power as G's increase in a turn. Just a little something to keep in mind as you inspect the wings in preflight

Overleaf This machine, 9GK, was originally owned by the US Navy, so it's properly called an SNJ. To the military, the only thing worse than surrender is for two service branches to share the same name for a common item

23

Above 'My airplane is made up of an SNJ-4 fuselage, a model D right wing and a model F left wing. The wings are attached to the fuselage by a total of 244 bolts. When I mated the wings, all but four bolts went in by hand. I tapped the four in lightly with a hammer', says Gordon. 'You can't appreciate how well it's built until you see it work'

Right Thirty seconds over Sausalito. The Golden Gate obliged with just enough maritime fog to make things interesting. The noise level was such that I couldn't hear my motor-driven cameras. Loud but smooth; the sound becomes background noise before long

What does he like most about it? 'It's my favourite seat in the whole world'. 9GK is a favourite among others as well. It took the Reseve Grand Champion prize at Oshkosh in 1986

Left Our camera aeroplane. Sister-ship T-6, owned by Jim Powers Sr and Jr, is also based at LVR. Shallow coordinated turns can be made without rudder as adverse yaw is minimal

Above Too soon, we're back on the ground. After shutdown, it's quiet. The RCAF colours hark back to the aeroplane's use in 1964 by the Harvard Aerobatic Team out of Moose Jaw, Saskatchewan

Above It's wise not to leave anything behind when you get out; retrieval can be tricky. The main gear struts use both air and oil to dampen shock. Tyre diameter is a load spreading 27 inches

Right Fill 'er up. The wing tanks together hold 110 US gallons of 80 octane avgas; 104 gallons usable. The engine's nine cylinders burn an average of 30 gallons per hour for an endurance of about 3.4 hours. The range is about 550 statute miles

'Under the cowling, it's dusty; nothing leaks. Once you buy a new part, you know it won't break. There's no real maintenance. Only my hard work keeping it clean and polished'

Opposite 'Parts are less expensive than Piper or Cessna parts and nothing important breaks anyway. When I get an annual inspection, the inspector examines the aeroplane for an hour and a half and says "OK"'

Below Handsome as they come, 9GK attracts a ground crew of admirers to help with the push back into the hangar. 5300 pounds of aeroplane doesn't roll around like a Piper Cub

Left All buttoned up. The hangar door closes on our adventure but not on the memory

Working Warbirds

Hooray for Hollywood! And airshows. If you don't own a warbird or live at an airport, then movies, television and airshows are the best outlets for warbird watching.

Shows in the air and on screen also do something else for warbirds. They help to keep them from drying up and blowing away. They generate and sustain interest. The resulting boost in demand motivates people to get and keep these machines in the air.

I'm sorry to report that if you could still 'pick up one of those babies in a crate for only $1500', they'd be long gone. At that rate, no one could afford to sit on aeroplanes and wait for people to come around and buy them. There would be more money left over after scrapping them.

Five, count 'em five! Duxford Airfield in June, 1989 was like a vein of gold for warbird enthusiasts. For those who came to see the aerial unit at work , the aeroplanes were the stars of the film

Above Ready to roll on her '24th mission' in the film's story line. Lucky film crew members got to suit up and go aloft, 'acting' as flight crew

Left 1943 going on '89. The B-17G *Sally B* wearing movie makeup for her title role as the *Memphis Belle*. Nose art was changed on some of the Flying Fortresses to enable the five assembled to pass for a greater number

Right Less glamorous roles were filled by others. These dedicated professionals were scripted to meet all manner of unsavoury ends

These pages The weathering applied to these usually pristine aeroplanes was convincing even in the flesh

Yeah, you're saying, but they're *soooo* expensive. I don't want to try arbitrating what's fair (whatever that is), so I'll stick to cold, hard numbers. Carl Scholl of Aero Trader at Chino estimates a single-engine fighter rebuild to take between four and ten thousand hours. The shop rate is $37.50 per hour. Don't forget to add in what you paid for your crate in the first place.

So far, this includes only labour. If a landing gear for your B-25 is on your shopping list, be prepared to dish out about $1000. A paint job can cost $20,000. Insurance can cost $15 per flight hour. You get the idea.

All is not bleak, however. The increasing equity tied up in these winged money pits is compelling motivation for their owners to take very good care of them. For all of us.

Left *Memphis Belle* camera ship was once a Tallmantz machine. Modified by movie flying giants Frank Tallman and Paul Mantz, this B-25 has seen some flying. The plexiglas in the nose has just one curve to keep distortion to a minimum. The view inflight gives panoramic a new meaning

Above Pilot Dizzy Addicott signalling a start for engine No 1 to ground crew with fire extinguisher. Yes, I went flying with someone named Dizzy

Above Dizzy and co-pilot Tony Ritzman taxi for take-off with a full load of film. The brown paper over the nose protects the plexiglas until the camera rolls. String is looped around the middle of the paper and passed through a small hole in the bottom of the plexiglas. When pulled from the inside, the string tears the paper which blows back and away

Right The Mitchell's tail is also fitted out for camera work. Don't drop anything you want to keep. At least there's no plexiglas to shoot through

Above *Memphis Belle* bad guys having a bit of hard luck. The Old Flying Machine Company's ex-Spanish Air Force HA.1112 Buchón (a licence-built Bf 109G), had its belly fuel tank come loose from its moorings. It's being drained so a repair can be made

Right A ciné camera gets fixed to the Buchón so Ray Hanna can fly some test shots for the director

Ray Hannah at the controls of OFMC's Mustang. Bomber crews called the
fighters their 'little friends'

Friend and foe share the same ramp during filming

Left The Battle of Britain Memorial Flight passes in review at Duxford in Cambridgeshire observing the 50th anniversary of the Battle. Not a dry eye in the house. While the Spitfire, Lancaster and Hurricane trio are always crowd pleasers, the impact seemed deeper that year

Above Murderers' row at Duxford's Classic Fighter Display. Starting with a dual controlled Spitfire, the line up is practically endless

Above Nick Grey eases into the cockpit of The Fighter Collection's Spitfire Mk IX during Air Fete '90 at RAF Mildenhall in Suffolk

Right OFMC's Spitfire Mk IX with Mark Hanna at the stick. MH434 is probably the most original airworthy Spitfire today. Built in August 1943, it was flown in 74 combat missions and accounted for five enemy aircraft destroyed. The airframe has never been rebuilt

Above Five blades plus one Rolls-Royce Griffon add up to a Spitfire PR.19. This example is one of two recce-Spitfires operated by the BBMF

Right The Hurricane's wooden waist saved war-scarce metal

Above Battle of Britain fighters were spotlighted at Air Fete 1990, with three Spitfires and two Hurricanes participating

Right George Ellis straps on The Shuttleworth Collection's Spitfire Mk Vc at Old Warden in Bedfordshire. The field's small scale makes for good close-in viewing

Preceding pages Exhaust was collected in pairs on this vintage. Three-bladed prop also speaks of relative rarity

Above The clouds part in time for . . .

Right . . . engine start and a prompt flattening of the grass. Spectators along the fence just behind are soon lightly flocked and no one minds a bit. 'I time my starts carefully; there's just five minutes from start-up to boil-over if I'm still on the ground', says George. The engine is under-radiated and needs a volume of cooling air that only flying speeds can provide

Above Tiger-mouthed P-40 taxis in after displaying at Duxford. Called the Warhawk in the US and Kittyhawk by Commonwealth forces, the P-40 excelled in the ground attack role after it became obsolete as a fighter

Right British fans know that a wing is sometimes most useful in affording protection from the rain. Not so in the glorious summer of 1990. That's an actual shadow under that Mustang's wing

Above P-51s are plentiful (compared to most other warbird types) because many were used for decades after World War 2 by air forces around the world. They left the military market after their value exceeded the scrap heap

Right Lars Ness stepping into the Scandinavian Historic Flight's Mustang. Aside from his parachute's more obvious benefit, the pilot's seat incorporates it as a cushion. Without it, even Lars' Viking frame would sit too low

Left 'It takes this many instruments to fly a Mustang', says Anders Saether of SHF. Loran and other modern additions have been kept to the sides of the cockpit, leaving the main panel for flying and engine instruments

Above Anders and Lars prepare to taxi SHF's Douglas A-26 Invader

Owner Gary Meermans gasses up
while Richard Reed battens down.
The Corsair is about to be flown at an
airshow at Hamilton Field in
California. An airline pilot, Gary likes
to show the aeroplane two weekends
a month in the summer

Left *Skyboss*, like so many warbirds displayed in the US, is not a commercial venture. Show organizers generally offer fuel to participants. You can arrive with your tanks only so empty and they won't stay full on the way home. It's a good way to have some flying underwritten but no way to make money

Above Hanging on for a while without breaking anything terribly expensive is turning into the surest way to make money, such has been the rate of appreciation in recent years. Of course that means parting with your machine in order to cash in

Racing

There's nothing to get your octane pumping like an air race. Warbirds are at the pinnacle of popularity among race classes these days. Even television, ever conscious of viewership numbers and therefore a good gauge of interest, is devoting more coverage.

It wasn't always so. Air racing was wildly popular in the 1920s and '30s. The aeroplane's novelty added to the excitement of the events; most spectators were seeing their first machines. Aircraft performance advanced at an astonishing rate and the Schneider, Bendix and Thompson trophy races were front page news.

After World War 2, the novelty was dimmed, the world had more serious concerns and a lot of people never wanted to see another aeroplane again. Airlines operated a glut of war surplus aircraft and aviation advances moved from the public eye to behind the closed doors of government and industry. Air racing did make a promising comeback in 1946 at Cleveland, Ohio but ended with a fatal accident involving non-spectators.

In 1964, air racing climbed out of the cellar at former racer Bill Stead's ranch outside Reno. Although the race circuit has grown, Reno remains the championship event.

Warbirds are to be found in the Unlimited and T-6/SNJ classes. Unlimiteds must have piston engines, be propeller driven and be capable of withstanding 6G. An aircraft turning with 80 degrees of bank pulls 5.76G and pylon racing is made of steep turns.

Engine and airframe modifications push the Unlimiteds well past their factory limits; often to the breaking point. Each competitor grapples with the fine balance of speed versus reliability. There are no points for running all but the last lap in first place. Lap speeds of nearly 470 mph are required to be competitive for the top prize.

The T-6/SNJ class allows far fewer changes to be made on the aeroplanes. The races are run essentially stock. Engines may be blueprinted; parts polished and set to but not exceeding factory specs. Seams are filled, rivets taped over and rear seats may be removed. The stock speed of 170 mph is increased to just over 230 mph for the contenders. The speed range among competitors is narrower than that of Unlimiteds, making for what some think is more exciting racing despite the lower speeds.

Right Find the cockpit in this picture. Normal amount of smoke at engine start momentarily obscures the outside world to the pilot

Both classes race over a span of four days preceded by qualifying. Results from qualifying and successive racing determine how the racers are slotted into heats for Bronze, Silver and Gold Trophies.

The races are started in the air with the field bossed by a pace aircraft. Timing officially starts when the first aircraft crosses the start/finish line. Races are closed course around pylons. Unlimited laps are just over nine miles and T-6/SNJ laps are a hair under five. From the time of take-off and forming up, running the race and landing, a pilot can be flying for something around 30 minutes—hot, loud, exhausting minutes.

Passing inside at pylons is not allowed and the overtaking aircraft must keep the other in sight. Overtaken machines can't interfere with their speedier competitors. Cutting inside a pylon draws a penalty of two seconds per number of laps in the race. Easily enough to put an offender out of the money.

Speaking of money. An unwritten rule is get bigger pockets so you can bring lots of it. Racing as a business is a push at best for the winner. There's only one winner.

Left Safely started, the ground crew can move off. Racing Corsair has clipped wings with straight tips. Shortening wings yields improved roll rates and lowers drag by reducing wetted surface. Since a certain minimum of wing area is needed just to get off the ground, there are limits to the available benefit

Above Their fingers are not in their ears to keep them warm. It's loud out there

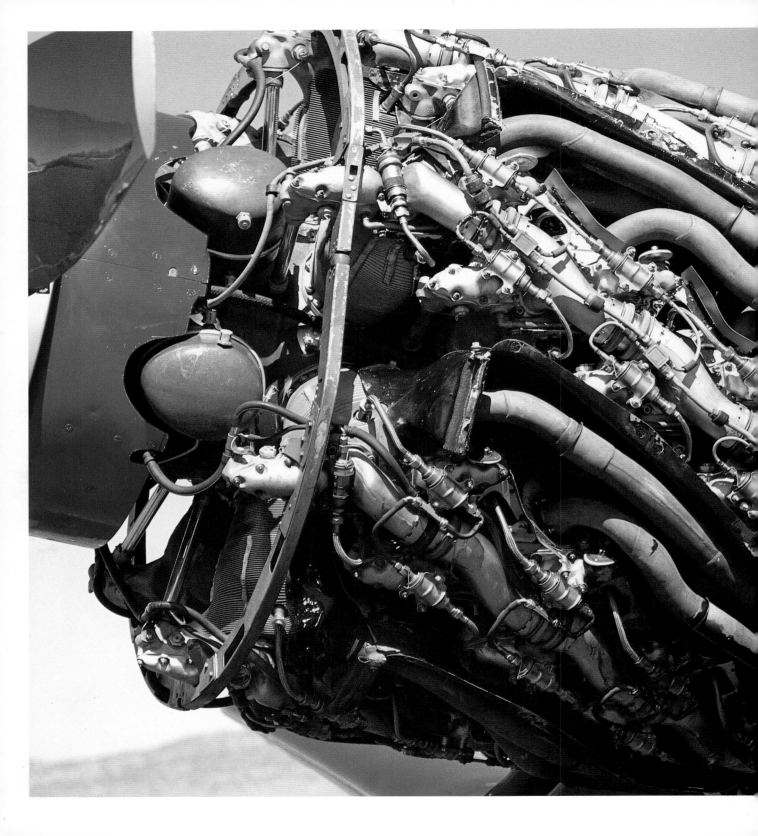

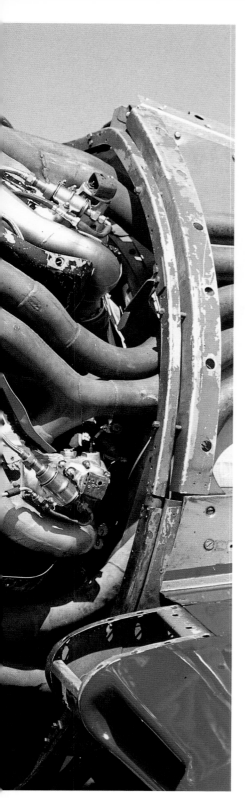

Left The R-4360 that hangs on the front of this Corsair is home and office for 56 spark plugs. It's easy to see where the corncob nickname comes from, with 28 cylinders in four rows. The DC-7 airliner was powered by four '4360s and, as you might guess, four Corsairs weigh a lot less than a DC-7

Above The Sea Fury is well represented in Unlimited racing. Eight of 36 out to qualify at Reno in 1990 were Sea Furies

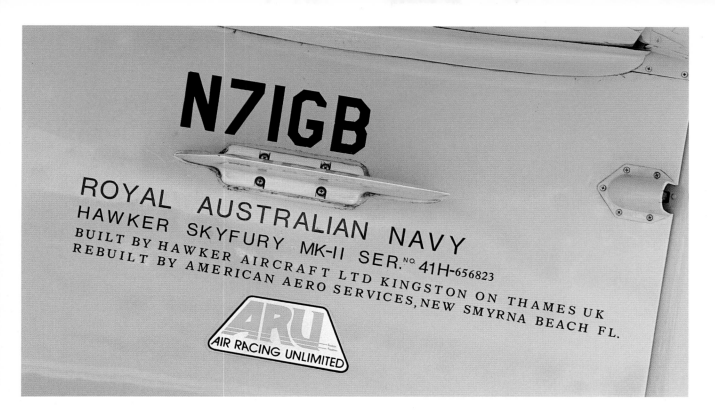

Above left It takes work to keep it this clean as the kitty litter on the ramp indicates. Oil has a habit of running along an aeroplane before dripping to the ground

Below left Drop tanks going on in preparation for the trip home. In this case Florida. The tanks will come in handy

Above Brief history tucked discreetly below the horizontal stabilizer

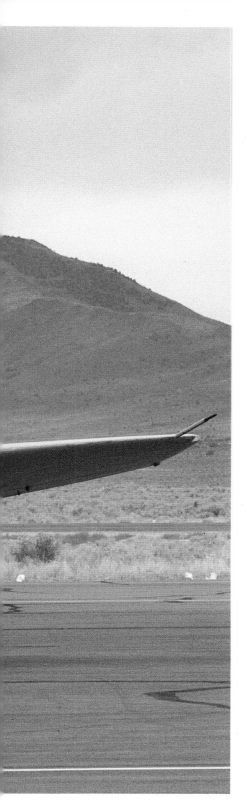

These pages *Baby Gorilla* runs up on the ramp. Tailhook doesn't help win races but looks good

One of the best seats in the pits. Jim Mott's Sea Fury is powered by a Bristol Centaurus; it clears the inside of the cowling by as little as $\frac{1}{8}$ inch

Best Tug Award had to go to P-40 *Spud Lag*. Practically everyone uses a pickup truck but this little gem did the job elegantly

These pages After hours fun. A pair of two-seat Mustangs get ready for some friendly formation flying

Left Legendary Lefty Gardner gets a handshake after winning Bronze heat 2C in P-51 *Thunderbird*. With his P-38 *White Lightning*, they made up 'The Thunder 'n Lightning Gang'

Above Turning money into noise

Left They spend more money painting a racer than you will on painting your house for the rest of your life

Above Aeroplanes compete with trailers for room in the pits. Workshop and storage space requirements seem to grow every year. It's a come-as-you-are sport and you have to come with more gear than you need or you'll surely need to have more

Left Water being pumped aboard *Miss Ashley*. That's right, water. It's sprayed into the radiator intake for much needed extra cooling. Water bed mattresses are used as bladders and are packed into ex-ammunition bays

Above He's not alone; just willing to proclaim. More than 150,000 people come to the races at Reno

Left Mustangs to the right of us, Mustangs to the left of us. A pit pass (anyone can buy one) is well worth it because it lands you smack in the middle of things. Workload permitting, the crew people will usually answer questions

Above Under the Big Top, *Strega* gets some TLC. Ask a Merlin mechanic what to do with a million dollars and the answer would probably be 'Tweak the engine 'till it was gone'

Left Cut-down canopy and waxing helps coax speed

Above Inside one of two *Strega* trailers, one of the many reasons why one trailer isn't enough. Jim Foss checks real-time engine data during a race. 'We watch for trends that can lead to trouble. It helps keep Tiger (Destefani's) head out of the cockpit', says Jim

Above left *Miss Fit* in between-race testing

Below left The tests pay off. Folks flock around after Erin Reinschild won the Bronze Trophy in *Miss Fit*

Above Erin's husband Bill, being interviewed by ESPN sports cable television after winning the Silver Trophy. Asked what he'd do following the victory he said, 'Pack up and enjoy the glow'. A warm glow, to be sure

These pages Thomas Camp holding a beer in one hand and the reason he's having it in the other. His Yak-11 had a bearing failure in its R-2800 engine, the pan contains the offending remnants. Yak's are becoming a 'cheap' alternative as former Eastern Bloc countries sell them off for Western (real) money

Above The observation deck is open and the crowd is going wild. The *Rare Bear* crew/entourage is cheering their Grumman on to victory for the Gold Trophy

Right Reno's answer to the victory lap. *Rare Bear* takes a bow in front of the grandstands before shutting down. The ramp is invaded with fans as soon as the prop stops. Lyle Shelton's winning speed was 468.620 mph

Overleaf No, you don't see one of these every day. Let alone get to walk right up to one. Lefty Gardner's P-38 is tuned for reliability rather than raceability so is not constantly roped off and covered with mechanics

These pages Lefty put on an aerial display that's always a hit

The Lockheed T-33's family tree is evident when comparing its nose with the P-38's. The jet was used as a pace aircraft for the flying start used in Unlimited racing. Steve Hinton did the honours

Above The forward line of the pits provide a good place to see the race, the ramp and the pits behind

Right Howard Pardue cranks around pylon No 2 in *Fury*. Wingtip vorticies reach the ground after the aeroplane passes and the engine's roar fades, stirring up the sagebrush like a poltergiest

Left It's not called Unlimited racing for nothing. With so many modifications available, the field stretches out and it becomes apparent who made the right choices. Most Unlimited heats are flown in trail after the first lap.

Above Robert Yancy's Yak-11 yanking and banking. Unlimited cockpit temperatures can reach 130 degrees Farenheit

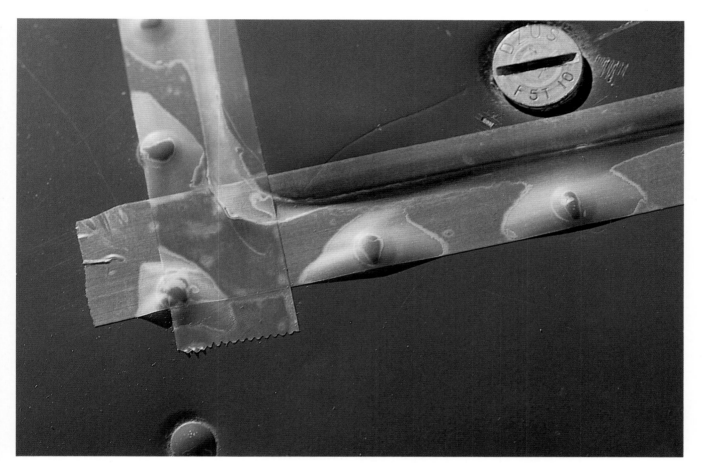

Left This Yak's R-2800 also tried to repeal the laws of physics

Above It's the little things that count. T-6ers leave no bump unfaired. How much good does it do? Tom Dwelle, owner/pilot of T-6 *Tinker Toy* says, 'It's good for 1/500 mph. When we do about 500 things like it, they start to make a difference'

These pages Running stock doesn't mean things stay adjusted forever

Alfred Goss begins his engine start checklist. Crewman stands by to remove battery cart after engine start

1989 RENO NATIONAL CHAMPION
AT-6 Closed Course
Record Holder 231.131 Avg.

1987 QUAL.
1988 QUAL.
1989 QUAL.

Above Hat gets swapped for a helmet before canopy closes. *Tinkertoy* was built for the RAF

Left Final Gold Trophy heat starts up in front of the grandstands instead of by the pits

Gene NcNeely with his head in the
cockpit

Above If you can't join 'em, watch 'em

Right *Yabba Dabba Doo* doing pylon No 6

Overleaf T-6/SNJ races look like races. The field stays together much more than do the Unlimiteds

With a field elevation of 5046 feet, you're already up in the clouds at Reno